if
Participant's
Guide

Participant's Guide

Trading Your *If Only* Regrets for God's *What If* Possibilities

Mark Batterson

BakerBooks

a division of Baker Publishing Group
Grand Rapids, Michigan

© 2015 by Mark Batterson

Published by Baker Books
a division of Baker Publishing Group
P.O. Box 6287, Grand Rapids, MI 49516-6287
www.bakerbooks.com

Printed in the United States of America

Library of Congress Cataloging-in-Publication Data is on file at the Library of Congress, Washington, DC.

ISBN 978-0-8010-1602-8

Some portions of this book have been adapted from *If: Trading Your If Only Regrets for God's What If Possibilities* (Baker, 2015).

Unless otherwise indicated, Scripture quotations are from the Holy Bible, New International Version®. NIV®. Copyright © 1973, 1978, 1984, 2011 by Biblica, Inc.™ Used by permission of Zondervan. All rights reserved worldwide. www.zondervan.com

Scripture quotations labeled KJV are from the King James Version of the Bible.

The author is represented by Fedd & Company, Inc.

15   16   17   18   19   20   21   7   6   5   4   3   2   1

Contents

Introduction

If.

It's a tiny two-letter word, but it's pregnant with possibilities.

There are 1,784 *ifs* in the Bible. Most of those *ifs* function as conditional conjunctions on the front end of God's promises. If we meet the condition, God delivers on the promise! So all that stands between your current circumstances and your wildest dreams is one little *if*.

One little *if* can change everything.

One little *if* can change anything.

For the next four weeks, we're going to study four *ifs*:

1. *If only* regrets
2. *As if* faith
3. *What if* dreams
4. *No ifs, ands, or buts about it* courage

If you stop and think about it, everything begins with *if*.

Every achievement, from the Nobel Prize to the Oscars, begins with *what if?* Every dream, from landing a man on the moon to the moon pies created to commemorate it, begins with *what if?* Every breakthrough, from the internet to iTunes, begins with *what if?*

So here's the question: What's your *what if?*

What gets you up early in the morning? What keeps you up late at night? What breaks your heart or makes your heart skip a beat? What puts a smile on your face? What makes you shed a tear? Those tears are clues. If you follow that trail of tears, it will lead you to your *what if.* So will the smile lines.

Think of this study as a jigsaw puzzle. Each session will reveal one piece of the puzzle. By the time we're done, you'll see the picture on the box top—your unique *what if.*

Session 1

If Only

Before watching Session 1 of the *If* DVD,
read chapters 1–7 in *If.*

Read, pray, and meditate on Romans 8:1–4:

> Therefore, there is now no condemnation for those who are in Christ Jesus, because through Christ Jesus the law of the Spirit who gives life has set you free from the law of sin and death. For what the law was powerless to do because it was weakened by the flesh, God did by sending his own Son in the likeness of sinful flesh to be a sin offering. And so he condemned sin in the flesh, in order that the righteous requirement of the law might be fully met in us, who do not live according to the flesh but according to the Spirit.

Write down your personal reflections.

_____

_____

_____

_____

_____

_____

_____

_____

_____

_____

_____

_____

_____

_____

_____

_____

_____

_____

_____

WHAT IF TIP

What if you read Romans 8 in several different translations? Check out the parallel feature on Biblehub.com. Try reading various translations side by side.

WATCH SESSION 1, PART 1

VIDEO NOTES

Watch the video for Session 1, Part 1. As you watch the video, use the following space to take notes.

_____

_____

_____

_____

_____

_____

_____

_____

_____

_____

_____

_____

Session 1

DISCUSSION QUESTIONS

1. Do you have a favorite coffeehouse? A favorite caffeinated drink of choice?

2. *If* opens with a story about Mark's life goal #102. Do you have a life goal list? Why or why not?

3. John Piper calls Romans 8 the greatest chapter in the Bible. Do you agree? What is your favorite chapter? Favorite verse?

4. Mark relates how Howard Schultz, CEO of Starbucks, reflected on the opportunity of a lifetime:

> *This is my moment*, I thought. *If I don't seize the opportunity, if I don't step out of my comfort zone and risk it all, if I let too much time tick on, my moment will pass.* I knew that if I didn't take advantage of this opportunity, I would replay it in my mind for my whole life, wondering: *What if?*[1]

Have you ever had a *what if* moment like that? Did you miss it or seize it?

5. The word *opportunity* comes from the Latin phrase *ob portu*. It was a nautical term that referred to the moment in time when the tide would turn. If a ship missed the turning of the tide, they'd have to wait for another tide to come in to ride into the harbor. Have you missed any opportunities that you regret?

6. One of Mark's maxims is this: *Don't seek opportunity—seek God, and then opportunity will seek you.* Are you seeking God first? Or are you seeking opportunity first?

7. What's your *what if*? Do you have a God-ordained passion or God-given dream that you'd be willing to share with the group?

PERSONAL REFLECTION

Take a few minutes to read and reflect on the following on your own. If possible, move apart from each other to minimize distractions before coming back together for Part 2 of this week's video.

Romans 8:31 is the hinge upon which the greatest chapter turns. It's the linchpin, the kingpin.

If God is for us, who can be against us?[2]

That verse is the game changer. But you've got to settle the issue. If you have subconscious doubts about God's good intentions, they'll manifest in a thousand forms of fear. But as 1 John 4:18 tells us, perfect love casts out all fear.

What if God is, in fact, for you? What if God is for you in every way imaginable—beyond your ability to ask or imagine? What if God is for you forever?

On a scale of 1 to 100, do you believe God is 100 percent for you—every day, in every way? Or do you have subconscious doubts? Where would you put yourself on a "holy confidence" scale?

1	10	20	30	40	50	60	70	80	90	100

If you have doubts, where do you think they come from?
Now let's dig a little deeper.
There are two primary traps we fall into.
The first trap is the *performance trap*. Simply put, how we feel about ourselves is tied more to our performance than to Christ's redeeming work on the cross. So we have ups and downs based on whether we're winning or losing the battle with sin. We forget that the penalty for our sin is paid in full, that our sins are nailed to the cross.

The only way out of the performance trap is coming to terms with the fact that your salvation is 100 percent by God's grace! Your performance has nothing to do with it—not even 1 percent. It's all

God. So we go all in and all out, not to *receive* God's grace but in *response* to God's grace.

The second trap is the *projection trap*. If you don't believe God is 100 percent for you, perhaps it's because you're not 100 percent for Him. Quit projecting your imperfections, your shortcomings, on God. He loves you perfectly, infinitely, and completely. There is nothing you can do to make God love you any more or any less. If you think God is holding out on you, perhaps it's because you're holding out on God.

The way out of the projection trap is the promises of God. When Christ died on the cross, He paid for every promise! Every promise is *yes* in Christ. God hasn't withdrawn His promises; we've withdrawn our faith.

Which trap do you fall into most frequently?

Is there a promise you need to start praying for, believing for?

_____

_____

_____

_____

_____

_____

_____

_____

WATCH SESSION 1, PART 2

VIDEO NOTES

Watch the video for Session 1, Part 2. As you watch the video, use the following space to take notes.

DISCUSSION QUESTIONS

1. If you could write your own eulogy, what would it say?

2. In the video, Mark talks about a study of fifty people over the age of ninety-five who were asked one question: *If you had your life to do over again, what would you do differently?* They said, "We would (1) risk more, (2) reflect more, and (3) do more things that live on after we die."

   Which comes more naturally to you, risking or reflecting?

3. This will require risk and reflection: share a regret with the group. What have you learned from it? How has God leveraged it?

4. Did you grow up in a family or a church that was more focused on sins of *commission* or sins of *omission*? How has that affected the way you view God, view life, and view yourself?

5. Mark makes a distinction between condemnation and conviction. Condemnation is feeling guilty over *confessed sin.* Conviction is feeling guilty over *unconfessed sin.*

Is it harder for you to *tune out* condemnation or *tune in* conviction?

6. If you don't listen to God's convicting voice, you won't hear His comforting voice or His guiding voice either. Hearing the voice of God is a package deal. If you don't listen to *everything* the Holy Spirit has to say, it's difficult to hear *anything* He has to say.

Do you agree or disagree? Why?

7. In the book, Mark talks about *the glass-half-empty gospel*. Mark says, "We tend to focus on the penalty for sin being paid, which is wonderful beyond words. But the righteousness of Christ has been credited to your account. So the glass isn't half empty; it's full of the righteousness of Christ. This half-empty mindset causes us to focus on forgiveness, but Jesus didn't die on the cross just to *forgive* you. His aim is much higher than that. He died to *change* you. And He didn't die on the cross just to keep you *safe*. He died to make you *dangerous*—a threat to the enemy. He died so that you could make a difference for all eternity."

What do you think is your default setting—settling for *forgiveness* or trying for *change*?

Are you a threat to the enemy? Or have you been playing it safe? What's the difference?

PERSONAL REFLECTION

Find an hour this week to read, reflect, and work through this week's "What If?" assignment.

When was the last time you searched your soul, ransacked your memory, or probed your motives?

A nebulous confession will result in a nebulous feeling of forgiveness.

A nuanced confession will result in a more nuanced sense of forgiveness.

Lamentations 3:23 says that God's mercies are new every morning. The English word *new* is the Hebrew word *hadas*. It doesn't just mean again and again. It's new as in *different*. It means *never before experienced*.

Today's mercy is different from yesterday or the day before or the day before the day before. Just as the seasonal flu vaccine changes from year to year, God's mercy changes from day to day. It's a new strain of mercy every day!

Now try this little exercise: Figure out how old you are—not in years, but in days.

What number did you come up with? _____

That is the sum total of unique mercies you've received, life-to-date. Take some time to nuance your gratitude to God.

WHAT IF?

Here's your assignment for this week: Find ten to fifteen minutes to write out a confession. You can use the following blank pages designed for tearing out of this book or your own paper or journal. Approach it like a stream of consciousness writing exercise, writing continuously for the allotted time. And don't forget to be *specific*. When you're done, don't just throw it away. Dispose of it in symbolic fashion—shred it, flush it, burn it, or deep-six it by giving it a burial at sea!

My Confession

_____

_____

_____

_____

_____

_____

_____

_____

_____

_____

_____

_____

_____

_____

_____

_____

As If

Before watching Session 2,
read chapters 8–14 in *If*.

Read, pray, and meditate on Romans 8:5–18:

Those who live according to the flesh have their minds set on what the flesh desires; but those who live in accordance with the Spirit have their minds set on what the Spirit desires. The mind governed by the flesh is death, but the mind governed by the Spirit is life and peace. The mind governed by the flesh is hostile to God; it does not submit to God's law, nor can it do so. Those who are in the realm of the flesh cannot please God.

You, however, are not in the realm of the flesh but are in the realm of the Spirit, if indeed the Spirit of God lives in you. And if anyone does not have the Spirit of Christ, they do not belong to Christ. But if Christ is in you, then even though your body is subject to death because of sin, the Spirit gives life because of righteousness. And if the Spirit of him who raised Jesus from the dead is living in you, he who raised Christ from the dead will also give life to your mortal bodies because of his Spirit who lives in you.

Therefore, brothers and sisters, we have an obligation—but it is not to the flesh, to live according to it. For if you live according to the flesh, you will die; but if by the Spirit you put to death the misdeeds of the body, you will live.

For those who are led by the Spirit of God are the children of God. The Spirit you received does not make you slaves, so that you live in fear again; rather, the Spirit you received brought about your adoption to sonship. And by him we cry, "*Abba*, Father." The Spirit himself testifies with our spirit that we are God's children. Now if we are children, then we are heirs—heirs of God and co-heirs with Christ, if indeed we share in his sufferings in order that we may also share in his glory.

I consider that our present sufferings are not worth comparing with the glory that will be revealed in us.

Write down your personal reflections.

_____

_____

_____

_____

_____

_____

_____

_____

_____

_____

_____

_____

_____

_____

_____

_____

_____

_____

_____

_____

_____

_____

_____

_____

_____

_____

_____

WHAT IF TIP

What if you used a pen to underline phrases, circle words, and write in the margins of your Bible?

WATCH SESSION 2

VIDEO NOTES

Watch the video for Session 2. As you watch the video, use the following space to take notes.

DISCUSSION QUESTIONS

1. In 1675, an actor named Mr. Butterton said to the Archbishop of Canterbury, "We actors on stage speak of things imaginary as if they were real, and you in the pulpit speak of things real as if they were imaginary."[3] While there are certainly exceptions, like George Whitefield, is this more true or less true today? Why or why not?

2. Mark describes one of his *what if* moments at Willow Creek Community Church. In *If,* he also shared the story of Congressman Tony Hall, whose *therefore* is ending world hunger. Have you ever had a moment like Mark or like Tony? A moment when your God-ordained purpose was revealed? A moment that made you mad or sad or glad—a moment that defines every other moment?

3. Mark says, "When we enter into a covenant relationship with God, we tend to focus on the fact that we are legally and morally bound to God, but God is also legally and morally bound to us. The gospel demands that we give all of ourselves to God, but when we do, God gives all of Himself to us." Do you tend to focus on your obligation to God or God's obligation to you?

4. In chapter 9 of *If*, Mark shares a unique definition of gratitude and faith. Gratitude is giving thanks *after* the blessing. Faith is giving thanks *before* the blessing. Which one are you better at? Is there something you need to thank God for, by faith, before it happens?

5. In Hebrews 11, the phrase *by faith* is repeated twenty-two times. You can't get where God wants you to go by logic. You can only get there *by faith*. Share with the group about a step of faith you've taken that wasn't logical, it was theological. What did you learn? Did you second-guess it?

6. Mark shares a few *as if* statements. If you had to rank them, which one are you best at? Which one do you most need to work on?

- "Pray as if everything depended on God. Work as if everything depended on you." —Saint Augustine

- "There are only two ways to live your life. One is as if nothing is a miracle. The other is as if everything is." —Albert Einstein

- "Live as if you were to die tomorrow. Learn as if you were to live forever." —Mahatma Gandhi

- "Treat a man as he is and he will remain as he is. Treat a man as he can be and should be and he will become as he can be and should be." —Johann Wolfgang von Goethe

7. John 1:14 says that Jesus was "full of grace and truth." Grace means I'll love you no matter what. Truth means I'll be honest with you no matter what. Grace without truth, or truth without grace, will erode a relationship. Healthy and holy relationships are grace-full and truth-full. In my experience, most people tend toward being truth oriented or grace oriented. Which do you tend toward? Do you more need to grow in grace or grow in truth?

PERSONAL REFLECTION

There are 31,102 verses in the Bible, and all of them point to the cross. The Old Testament points forward while the New Testament points backward. But either way, the cross is the reference point.

Charles Haddon Spurgeon had a famous maxim: *make a beeline for the cross*. That motto is true in any and every circumstance. It outranks every adage, outlasts every axiom. One way of doing that is communion.

Hold that thought.

The word *remember* is repeated no less than 148 times in Scripture.[4]

Remember the Sabbath day, to keep it holy.[5]

Remember the days of old.[6]

Remember the wonders he has done.[7]

Remember Lot's wife![8]

But the most significant *remember*, in my opinion, is the one Jesus said at the Last Supper: "Do this in remembrance of me."[9]

Take a few minutes on your own to *remember*.

Optional: Celebrate communion together as a group. (If a pastor administers communion in your church tradition, ask them to join you for this part of the study.) There is no more powerful *as if* than the bread and the cup. The bread represents the body of Christ. The cup represents the precious blood of Christ. When you celebrate communion, it's a renewal of the covenant relationship you have with God. It's a reminder of your obligation to God, and God's obligation to you.

One of our fundamental problems is living as if Christ is still nailed to the cross. He's not. He's seated at the right hand of the Father, in power and glory. The only thing nailed to the cross is our sin. And the hammer of God's mercy has no claw. Once your sin is nailed, it's nailed.

WHAT IF?

Here is this week's assignment: Make a gratitude list or goal list.

A gratitude list is thanking God for the things He has done—past tense.

A goal list is believing God for what He's going to do—future tense.

Try to come up with twenty-five gratitudes or goals.

1. _____
2. _____
3. _____
4. _____
5. _____
6. _____
7. _____
8. _____
9. _____
10. _____
11. _____
12. _____
13. _____

14. _____
15. _____
16. _____
17. _____
18. _____
19. _____
20. _____
21. _____
22. _____
23. _____
24. _____
25. _____

What If

Before watching Session 3,
read chapters 15–26 in *If*.

Read, pray, and meditate on Romans 8:20–33:

For the creation was subjected to frustration, not by its own choice, but by the will of the one who subjected it, in hope that the creation itself will be liberated from its bondage to decay and brought into the freedom and glory of the children of God.

We know that the whole creation has been groaning as in the pains of childbirth right up to the present time. Not only so, but we ourselves, who have the firstfruits of the Spirit, groan inwardly as we wait eagerly for our adoption to sonship, the redemption of our bodies. For in this hope we were saved. But hope that is seen is no hope at all. Who hopes for what they already have? But if we hope for what we do not yet have, we wait for it patiently.

In the same way, the Spirit helps us in our weakness. We do not know what we ought to pray for, but the Spirit himself intercedes for us through wordless groans. And he who searches our hearts knows the mind of the Spirit, because the Spirit intercedes for God's people in accordance with the will of God.

And we know that in all things God works for the good of those who love him, who have been called according to his purpose. For those God foreknew he also predestined to be conformed to the image of his Son, that he might be the firstborn among many brothers and sisters. And those he predestined, he also called; those he called, he also justified; those he justified, he also glorified.

What, then, shall we say in response to these things? If God is for us, who can be against us? He who did not spare his own Son, but gave him up for us all—how will he not also, along with him, graciously give us all things? Who will bring any charge against those whom God has chosen? It is God who justifies.

Write down your personal reflections.

_____

_____

_____

_____

_____

_____

_____

_____

_____

_____

_____

_____

_____

_____

_____

WHAT IF TIP

Memorize your favorite verse in your favorite translation.

VIDEO NOTES

Watch the video for Session 3. As you watch the video, use the following space to take notes.

DISCUSSION QUESTIONS

1. Have you ever made a bold prediction? Or a bad prediction? Or perhaps someone has made a prediction about you? Share it with the group.

2. For better or for worse, our words become self-fulfilling prophecies. Do you have a "Say Not" list? Is there something you need to put on this list?

3. You were once an idea in the mind of almighty God—you are the physical manifestation of God's eternal plans and purposes. Simply put, you are God's *what if*. How does that change the way you see yourself and see others?

4. Mark shares his definitions of *doubt* and *faith*. Doubt is putting your circumstances between you and God. Faith is putting the promises of God between you and your circumstances. Share an experience where you did one or the other.

5. In Romans 16, Paul shares his who's who list—his upline and downline. Who's on your who's who list?

6. Have you ever had a God idea? What was it? How did you know it was a God idea, not just a good idea?

7. Mark says, "Sometimes faith can be measured in dollars." Do you agree or disagree? Share a financial step of faith you've taken.

PERSONAL REFLECTION

The ancient Greek mathematician Archimedes of Syracuse once said: "Give me a place to stand, and I will move the earth."[10] It's called the law of the lever. Simply put, a lever amplifies input force to provide greater output force. The longer the lever, the greater the leverage.

In any system, there is something called the high leverage point. It's the place in a system's structure where a small amount of change force can cause a large change in the system's behavior. It's the one change that can change everything.

You are one decision away from a totally different life. It'll probably be the toughest decision you've ever made. But it can leverage the rest of your life!

The spiritual disciplines are high leverage points.

Rank the following disciplines from 1 to 5, with 1 being the discipline you practice most regularly, most effectively:

____ Studying Scripture

____ Praying

____ Journaling

____ Meditating

____ Fasting

WHAT IF?

This week's assignment is to take one of the disciplines and leverage it. Try fasting or journaling or meditating for one week. Set the parameters before starting—what you'll fast from, how much you'll write, or how long you'll meditate. Then put it into practice every day for seven days. After ending the experiment, evaluate it. Then take that discipline to the next level or try leveraging a new one.

No Ifs, Ands, or Buts about It

Before watching Session 4,
read chapters 27–30 and the epilogue in *If*.

Read, pray, and meditate on Romans 8:34–39:

> Who then is the one who condemns? No one. Christ Jesus who died—more than that, who was raised to life—is at the right hand of God and is also interceding for us. Who shall separate us from the love of Christ? Shall trouble or hardship or persecution or famine or nakedness or danger or sword? As it is written:
>
>> "For your sake we face death all day long;
>>   we are considered as sheep to be slaughtered."
>
> No, in all these things we are more than conquerors through him who loved us. For I am convinced that neither death nor life, neither angels nor demons, neither the present nor the future, nor any powers, neither height nor depth, nor anything else in all creation, will be able to separate us from the love of God that is in Christ Jesus our Lord.

Write down your personal reflections.

_____

_____

_____

_____

_____

_____

_____

_____

_____

_____

_____

_____

_____

_____

_____

_____

_____

_____

WHAT IF TIP

Choose a verse, any verse, and try meditating on it for ten to fifteen minutes. Then journal your thoughts by jotting down questions, making observations, or turning a promise into a prayer.

VIDEO NOTES

Watch the video for Session 4. As you watch the video, use the following space to take notes.

Session 4

_____

_____

_____

_____

_____

_____

_____

_____

_____

_____

_____

_____

_____

_____

_____

_____

DISCUSSION QUESTIONS

1. Scientific researchers point to "We Are the Champions" as the catchiest song in popular music. What's your current favorite or all-time favorite song? If you're feeling brave, sing a line of lyrics.

2. A. W. Tozer said, "What comes into our minds when we think about God is the most important thing about us."[11] Do you agree? What comes to mind for you?

3. Do you pray as if Jesus is still on the cross or as if He is seated at the right hand of the Father?

4. Is there someone who has been "in your corner"—someone who believed in you more than you believed in yourself? Who was it? How has it changed your life?

5. More than a hundred years ago, General William Booth, the founder of the Salvation Army, said, "The chief dangers which confront the coming century will be religion without the Holy Ghost, Christianity without Christ, forgiveness without repentance, salvation without regeneration, politics without God, heaven without hell."[12] What's your reaction to that statement? Is it still true?

6. In the final chapter of *If*, "Keep Calm and Carry On," Mark writes about a moment when he found himself between the Egyptian army and the Red Sea. Have you ever found yourself in that kind of situation? Share it with the group.

7. As we near the end of this study, which verse in Romans 8 is your personal favorite?

PERSONAL REFLECTION

There is an old adage: "Let your conscience be your guide." Mark one-ups it by saying, "Let your *convictions* be your guide." He then shares a few of his kernels of truth, his core convictions:

Pray like it depends on God and work like it depends on you.

Criticize by creating.

Thou shalt offend Pharisees.

Catch people doing something right.

Playing it safe is risky.

If you stay humble and stay hungry, there is nothing God cannot do through you.

If you don't know what your convictions are, you don't really know *who* you are. Your convictions are the truest thing about you. You are your convictions. Or more accurately, you become your convictions.

What are your core convictions?

What are you willing to die for?

What are your *no ifs, ands, or buts about it* convictions?

WHAT IF?

Here's your last assignment: Come up with a list of your core convictions. It's okay to borrow some ideas from others—including Mark's maxims—but make sure you personalize them. Do an inventory of your past. What are the maxims, the sayings, the axioms you were taught by your family, your coaches, your teachers? Which promises do you quote most frequently?

Notes

1. Howard Schultz and Dori Jones Yang, *Pour Your Heart into It: How Starbucks Built a Company One Cup at a Time* (New York: Hyperion, 1997), 63.

2. Romans 8:31.

3. John Rinehart, *Gospel Patrons* (Reclaimed Publishing, 2013), 63.

4. That is, in the King James Version.

5. Exodus 20:8 KJV.

6. Deuteronomy 32:7.

7. Psalm 105:5.

8. Luke 17:32.

9. Luke 22:19.

10. See "The Lever: Introduction," http://www.math.nyu.edu/~crorres/Archimedes/Lever/LeverIntro.html. Accessed March 18, 2015.

11. A. W. Tozer, *The Knowledge of the Holy: The Attributes of God: Their Meaning in the Christian Life* (New York: HarperOne, 2009), 1.

12. "William Booth," Salvation Army Torrance Corps, 2015, http://www1.usw.salvationarmy.org/usw/www_usw_torrance2.nsf/vw-sublinks/FCD98CD6A8BFB1B68825771D00178DE1?openDocument.

Mark Batterson is the *New York Times* bestselling author of *The Circle Maker*, *The Grave Robber*, and *A Trip around the Sun*. He is the lead pastor of National Community Church, one church with seven campuses in Washington, DC. Mark has a doctor of ministry degree from Regent University and lives on Capitol Hill with his wife, Lora, and their three children. Learn more at www.mark batterson.com.

Connect with

MARK
BATTERSON
at
MarkBatterson.com

 @MarkBatterson

Mark Batterson

@MarkBatterson

Connect with National Community Church at
WWW.THEATERCHURCH.COM

LIVE YOUR *WHAT IF* POSSIBILITIES

If is a powerful little word. Why?
Because the answer to "If God is for us, who
can be against us?" is "No one." God is always
on our side. Every day, in every way.

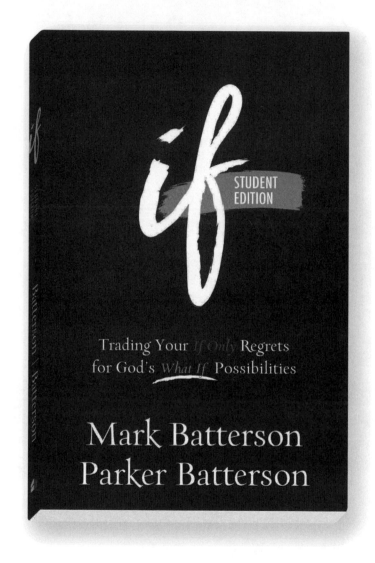

WHAT IF GOD IS FOR US?